INTRODUCTION

In recent years, there has been an upsurge in the number of people who have chosen a cat above other pets to share their home with. This trend is likely to continue into the future because the cat offers many advantages when compared to just about all other domestic companions. It is small, extremely clean in its personal habits, economic to feed, or screeching as may the larger parrots. It can be allowed the freedom of your garden without the worry it will chase children. It is a reclusive creature by nature and likes to keep to itself.

I do not suggest the cat is the perfect pet for everyone because there are those who do not like its natural habit of catching young birds and other animals—but

Geri's Kissin' Ana Huggin', a blue point Himalayan owned by Geri Hamilton, is a picture perfect feline.

very affectionate to its owner, and with sound care and a little luck, may well live to reach an age of 20 or more years.

Unlike rabbits, guinea pigs, and other small pets, it does not need to be caged, nor is it likely to offend your neighbors by howling when you are away as dogs might those same people would no doubt be very thankful to see it keeping rats and mice away from their property. There are others who view the cat as a pet that is beyond being trained to respond to its owner as will a dog. If you are the sort who insists on dominating everything in your home, then you probably would not find a cat an ideal companion.

If on the other hand you can love an animal that displays an independence of character and one that will return affection with affection on an equal basis, a cat would be the perfect pet. It makes few demands of its owner and expects few to be made of it. The cat is basically a solitary animal, whereas the dog is from a highly social background. These important natural differences give each their appeal to those who keep them. Many pet owners delight in keeping both and find them ideal companions for each other and for the human members of the household.

If you have decided that a cat is the pet for you, there are many questions that you may need answered before you make your final selection. This book is devoted to those who think they would like a Himalayan. However, much of the text has equal application to any cat and particularly to those which are longhaired. These latter felines have special needs directly as a result of their gorgeous coat, so it should not be assumed that because you want a Himalayan it is the ideal breed for your particular situation.

In the following chapters, you will find all the answers to the questions you are likely to be

Although the cat isn't the perfect pet for everyone, the Himalayan's gentle disposition and lovable character can make a cat lover out of almost anyone.

Himalayans make excellent show cats. They are extremely popular with exhibitors and competition within the breed is always intense.

asking yourself about this breed. You will be aware of the many attributes of this majestic cat and also of the responsibilities that go with it. It is hoped you will go ahead and purchase a Himalayan, but if you feel after reading the book that you do not think you would be wise to own the breed, the text will have been equally worthwhile. When choosing any feline, it is important that it is suited to your particular character. Essentially, it comes down to whether or not you are prepared to commit to the grooming needs of any longhaired breed. If not, do not despair. There are numerous alternatives that will meet your needs and allow you to have a cat that sports the famous Himalayan coat pattern. These too will be cited so that you are not left wondering what your alternatives are.

If you are interested in showing or breeding cats, the Himalayan is an excellent choice. It is highly popular with exhibitors, and competition is always extremely keen. It is also available in a number of coat colors and will appeal to those who enjoy the challenge of color breeding.

BREED HISTORY

The ancestry of the Himalayan breed combines the genes of the two most important cat breeds in respect to the number of other breeds each has produced. However, before we look at how the Himmy, as it is affectionately known, became a breed, it is perhaps worthwhile to briefly retrace the complete development of the cat as a domestic pet. To do this we must travel back in time to the days of the ancient Egyptians.

WILD CATS BECOME TAME

Whether or not the Egyptians were the first people to domesticate the cat remains unproved, but without any doubt, they must be credited with its subsequent establishment and elevation to that of a cherished house pet. The first strong indications that the cat was truly a domestic animal in Egypt date back to about 2300 B.C., towards the end of the Old Kingdom. As we come forward in time, more and more artifacts indicate the growing importance of the cat to the peoples of the Nile Delta.

Himalayan, Pointed Pattern Persian, or Colorpoint Longhair? What you call the breed depends on personal choice or registry membership, but, whatever the name, the fact remains that you own a startlingly beautiful and colorful longhaired cat.

The domestic cat is thought to have been developed from the wild feline species known as the African wild cat, *Felis libyca*, with possibly some genes being contributed by another small wild *felis* called the jungle cat, *Felis chaus*. Some zoologists regard each of these species as being subspecies of the European wild cat, *Felis sylvestris*. The reason the cat was adopted by the Egyptians was not initially for its companionship— this came later. The cat's great value was in helping control the growing mice and rat populations that were feasting on the increasing quantities of grain that the Nile people were harvesting to sustain their own growing numbers.

So important was this role, that eventually the cat was regarded as an earthly form of one of the many Egyptian gods. By about 1500 B.C., the cat goddess Bast, or Bastet, was becoming a very important goddess in the hierarchy of the Egyptian pantheon. By the time of the Libyan kings (1070-712 B.C.),

The Himalayan has been recognized as a distinct breed for only a relatively short time. However, the history of its ancestry dates back to early Egypt and possibly 16th century Russia or Turkey.

Bast was possibly the most worshipped of all Egyptian gods and with some people even ahead of the pharaohs themselves. Cat worship remained a key part of Egyptian life until it was, along with all other national gods, banned by the Romans in A.D. 390. But by that time, the cat had been exported to Greece and Rome where it was to be held in high esteem, even though its status may not have been as elevated as that of former times.

The all-conquering Roman armies transported the cat to most mainland European countries, thence to Britain. From the latter, as well as from Spain, Holland, and Portugal, the domestic feline was taken to all parts of the world on the sailing ships of these nations.

THE ORIGIN OF LONGHAIRED BREEDS

Surprisingly, there is no record of any longhaired cats until about the 16th century, when they became evident in wood engravings and other art forms seen in Italy and elsewhere in Europe. There is also speculation as to whether the gene mutation that creates long hair derived from a country such as Russia or from the higher altitudes of more southerly countries like Turkey, Persia (now Iran), and Afghanistan.

Whatever the origin, it is clear that in Russia and Turkey the longhaired cat became highly valued and was selectively bred to improve its coat. Examples were taken back to Europe by soldiers

and other travelers. These cats became very fashionable, especially with the nobility of European countries with whom they were often depicted in paintings.

Although there were at least two quite distinct longhaired cat types as the 19th century unfurled, the distinction between them became more blurred with the passage of further years. The dense and more woolly coat of Persian type cats was preferred by breeders of the day to the silky, more flowing coat of the Turkish felines. Interbreeding eventually resulted in the Persian type being the preeminent longhaired cat. Along with selection for an ever denser coat, breeders also showed preference for a more cobby cat and one with a rounder face that featured large round eyes. The modern day Persian was so created. In more recent years, the Turkish type in the form of the Angora and the Van has been reestablished.

THE RISE OF THE SIAMESE

At the World's first cat show in London during 1871, there appeared what was at that time a most unusual feline. It had dark brown extremities and a lighter colored body. Today that breed, the Siamese, is of course known to just about everybody regardless of whether or not they keep cats. It became extremely popular with exhibitors and rapidly rose to the top of the breed charts. Only the Persian prevented it from becoming the most popular cat in the world. Along with the Persian,

The Himalayan is a wonderful mix of the Persian and Siamese in appearance, although it most resembles the Persian in its gentle disposition.

the Siamese was to be used in the development of numerous other breeds. Its special color pattern was what most breed developers wanted, but the fact that it also possessed a very unique character did not go unnoticed either. Clearly, sooner or later, someone would try to combine the color pattern of the Siamese with the gorgeous longhair of the Persian. This was achieved, and the result is the breed we know as the Himalayan. If you wonder why it was called the Himalayan, it is because of the pointed pattern on its body. Other animals also display this pattern, such as, the rabbit, the guinea pig, and the mouse, to name but three.

THE HISTORY OF THE HIMALAYAN CAT

The first attempts to combine the Siamese and Persian genes can be traced to both Sweden and the USA during the years 1920-45, but the various breeders involved failed to establish a breed. In 1947, Brian Stirling-Webb, an English breeder, took up the challenge. He and his wife acquired cats that possessed the required genetic background from other experimental breeders. This time success came. In 1955, the Governing Council of the Cat Fancy (GCCF) of Britain accepted the new breed and gave it the name Colourpoint Longhair.

Meanwhile in the USA and Canada, breeders were also trying to establish the same breed. Using British imports as well as stock produced in North America, success was again achieved. Official recognition commenced with the American Cat Fanciers Association in 1958. Within the next few years, all other American registries adopted standards for the new breed, which was called the Himalayan.

The status of the breed today depends upon which association you are a member. In Britain, the term Persian was dropped for some years, and all longhaired cats of Persian type were simply called longhaired with each color being given breed status. The Himalayan remained as one of these under the name of Colourpoint Longhair. Today, the Colourpoint is classed under the now revived name of Persian longhairs. In the USA, the Himalayan was given separate breed status from the Persian. However, in 1984, the Cat Fanciers Association (CFA), America's largest cat registry,

determined that the Himalayan would no longer be regarded as a breed apart from the Persian rather as a variety of it. It is now classified as the Pointed Pattern Persian.

This decision was based on very sound genetic theory. The Himalayan was judged according to the standard of the Persian except with Siamese patterned points (mask, ears, tail, and legs). Once the breed had been established, there was no need to mate Himmies to Siamese, so Himmy to Himmy was the standard pairing. This, however, resulted in a loss of Persian type over a number of generations. Himmy to Persian matings were thus practiced in order to regain type. Any Siamese genes, other than those for the color pattern, have long since been diluted to the degree that they can be regarded as non existent in the breed, which is now as Persian as any other color variety within the breed.

Other associations in the USA will either regard the Himalayan as a Persian variety or as a separate breed. If a Himmy is mated to a solid-colored Persian, the result will be all solid colored kittens, but they will carry the genes for Himmy pattern. In those associations that regard the Himalayan as a variety of the Persian, such kittens would be classified as colorpoint carriers. If these were paired together, a percentage of their offspring would be pure Himalayan patterned, while the rest would be either pure solid-colored Persian or solid-colored colorpoint carriers.

Whether you call this breed a Colourpoint Longhair, a Pointed Pattern Persian, or a Himalayan is a matter of personal choice or registry membership. All are the same breed, and all Himalayans are judged according to the Persian standard. Some owners claim that the breed still retains certain of the characteristics of the Siamese, but this is unlikely given the number of generations of Himalayan to Persian matings involved. The Himalayan has the gentle disposition of the Persian, which can be regarded as the most domesticated of any cat breed.

Much of the Himalayan's type and temperament come from its Persian background. Persian genes also give the Himalayan its beautiful long hair.

Siamese and Persians were bred together to produce the breed now known as the Himalayan. The Himalayan gets its colorful points from Siamese genes.

SELECTING

Before discussing the matter of selecting a Himalayan cat or kitten, it is appropriate to offer a cautionary note. The Himalayan is a singularly beautiful feline with a magnificent coat. However, this coat is not self-grooming! If left unattended the Himalayan can look a very sorry example of a cat. The fur will mat right down to the daily to ensure the coat remains in the best condition.

THE QUALITY OF YOUR PET

Himalayans come in a range of qualities from the inferior, through the typical examples of the breed, to those which are show winners, or at least potentially so. You may wish to

Most breeders won't part with kittens until they are at least ten weeks of age because it is safer for the kittens to remain with their mother for that time period.

skin. The extent of the mats will become greater every time your pet gets wet. If you are not prepared to devote at least 20 or so minutes every other day to grooming your Himalayan, then do not obtain an example of this breed (or indeed any longhaired breed). If you plan to exhibit your Himalayan, it will need grooming own a high-quality Himalayan even though you have no intention to show it. Quality means it will have good bone conformation, the correct stature, and its color or patterns will be of a high standard. Such a cat will be a costly purchase. A typical Himalayan will be just that. It will display no glaring faults, and its

The Himalayan is a beautiful longhaired breed that needs much grooming attention. If you can't devote the time to grooming, the Himalayan is the wrong cat for you.

color will be sound. It may display some minor failings in type or color that would preclude it from ever being of show quality.

An inferior Himalayan will be one which has obvious faults, either its conformation, its coat quality, poor color or in other ways inferior. Such cats are often described as being pet quality. As long as you appreciate that this term means inferior, its use is fine. However, there are two kinds of inferior Himalayans. There is the cat which is inferior only in respect to its type and color—not in relation to its basic structure and health.

There is then the inferior cat produced by those who are in Himalayans just to make money. These people have cats that they breed with no consideration for the vigor of the offspring. Such kittens are invariably sickly and prone to illnesses throughout their lives. Poor health and inferior Himalayans result from unplanned matings and excessive breeding, coupled with a lack of ongoing selection being applied to future breeding stock.

How do you make the right choice when selecting a Himalayan? The answer is you do your homework. Visit shows, talk to established exhibitors, and judges. When you visit the seller take a good look at his stock, and more especially the living conditions of the cats. Is he giving you the hard sell, or does he seem more concerned about the kitten's future home? Sometimes the

If you decide to become a breeder of Himalayan cats, then a female is a much better choice than a male. GRC and GRP Purrstar's Somethin' Elsa, owned by Barbara Leffler.

If you enjoy the antics of kittens at play, you may want to bring home two kittens instead of one. They will keep you amused and they will keep each other company when you are not home.

dedicated seller might even annoy you, but he is concerned for his kittens, even if they are not quality Himalayans. The more Himalayans you see, the more likely you are to make a wise choice.

WHICH SEX TO PURCHASE?

From the viewpoint of pet suitability, there really is no difference between a tom (male) and a queen (female). Some people prefer one sex, but this is purely subjective. This author has found males to be more consistent in their character than females, who may tend to be "all or nothing" in their attitude. In other words, they can be extremely affectionate one day, but rather standoffish the next. The tom tends to be much the same from one day to the next, whatever his character might be.

It really is a pot-luck matter just how affectionate a kitten will grow up to become. Cats are very much individuals, and they can change as they grow up. The way they are treated also affects their personality. Therefore, it is more a case of selecting a kitten that appeals to you, regardless of its sex.

Of course, if you wish to become a breeder then the female has to be the better choice. Once she reaches breeding age you can then select a suitable mate for her from the hundreds of quality stud males available to you. If you purchase a male with the view to owning a stud, you are really gambling that he will mature into a fine cat that others would want to use. For this to happen, your tom would need to be very successful in the show ring, and then in the quality of his offspring.

Furthermore, owning a whole tom (a male that has not been neutered) does present more practical problems than owning a queen. Such a male will be continually marking his territory (your furniture) by spraying it with his urine, which is hardly a fragrant scent!

If your Himalayan is to be a pet only, then regardless of the sex you should have it neutered or spayed. It will be more affectionate to you, will not be wandering off looking for romance, and will not shed its coat as excessively as would an unaltered Himalayan. In the case of a tom, he will not come home with pieces of his ears missing as a result of his fights with other entire males. Your queen will not present you with kittens that you do not want but which she will have if she is not spayed. She is far less likely to spray than is the male, but she will show her desire to mate, both with her "calling" sounds, which can be eerie, and her provocative crouching position in which she is clearly inviting a mating.

WHAT AGE TO PURCHASE?

Breeders vary in the age they judge a kitten ready for a new home. An important consideration is obviously if the new owners have experience of cats generally and kittens in

particular. While an eight-week-old baby is quite delightful, it is invariably better from a   health standpoint that the kitten remains with its mother until it is ten or more weeks of age. Some breeders will not part with a kitten until it is 16 weeks of age.

The kitten should have received at least temporary vaccinations against feline distemper and rabies (if applicable in your country and if the kitten is over 12 weeks of age) and preferably protection against other major feline infections. Additionally, you should let your own vet examine your Himalayan.

Although most owners will wish to obtain a kitten, a potential breeder or exhibitor may find that a young adult (over eight to nine months of age) is more suitable to his needs. By this age the quality of the Himalayan is becoming more apparent. However, bear in mind that a mature Himalayan queen will not be at her peak until she is about two years of age. A tom will be even later in reaching full maturity, and he may not peak until he is five years of age.

ONE OR TWO HIMALAYANS?

Without any doubt, two kittens are always preferred to one. They provide constant company for each other and are a delight to watch as they play. The extra costs involved in their upkeep are unlikely to be a factor if you are able to afford a Himalayan in the first place.

Himalayans, like Persians, are irresistible as kittens. You should make your selection based on health and temperament traits rather than just on color.

GENERAL CARE & GROOMING

In order to properly care for your Himalayan kitten, it is advisable to purchase certain essential items before it arrives in your home. You will want at least one large litter tray. If it is too small, you will only need a bigger one later. Trays can be of the simple open style or domed to retain the odor within them.

freestanding models that can be simple or very complex climbing frames. A third essential will be a cat carrier, which can be fiberglass or of the metal cage type. Apart from being a means of transporting kitty to the vet, it also doubles as a bed and a place to confine a kitten if necessary.

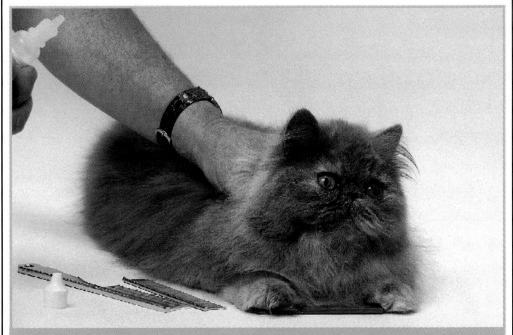

For a longhaired cat, grooming is an essential part of keeping it healthy. Longhaired breeds have a tendency to look unkempt if not groomed at least every other day.

You can also purchase a litter tray curtain so that the tray is discreetly hidden yet accessible for your kitty. You will need a bag of cat litter as well.

Another essential item will be a scratching post, otherwise your cat will shred your furniture. Posts come in a range of styles—from those that are fitted to the wall to the

You will need a soft hand brush, preferably of natural bristle not nylon, as well as one or more combs. Again, nylon is not the best choice for a comb because it generates static electricity that causes the hair to "fly." One comb should be wide-toothed, the other medium or narrow. As the kitty grows up, an extra brush of a more stiff

A light brushing at the end of a grooming session removes the final bits of dead hair from your Himalayan's coat.

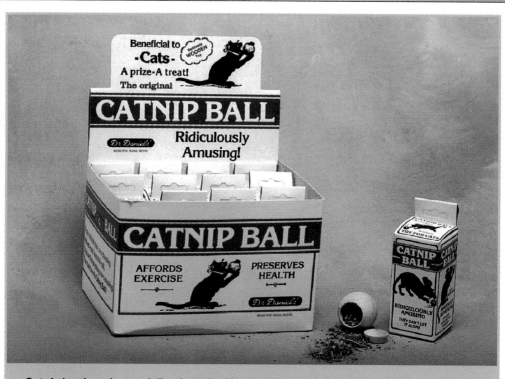

Catnip has long been a feline favorite. Now available in many different forms, this treat is popular among cats. Photo courtesy of Dr. A. C. Daniels.

bristle type will be required. Although it may not be needed initially, you will eventually need an elasticized cat collar and name tag.

You will also need feeding utensils: a food bowl and water bowl. There is a wide variety of them available at pet shops. Finally, your new kitten will enjoy play toys. Balls and "squeaky" mice seem to be favorites with many cats.

SAFETY PRECAUTIONS

Before the kitten arrives in your home, check that there are no safety hazards. An open balcony is an obvious risk, as are any trailing electrical wires that are always left in their sockets. A washing machine with the door left open is a tempting place for a kitten to take a catnap. Always be careful where open doors and windows are concerned. Apart from the kitten running out if the door is an outside exit, there is the danger of doors slamming on the kitten.

Be very careful when kitty is in the kitchen and you are working. They have a habit of always being under your feet as you turn round. Should you be carrying a boiling hot saucepan, this could be a real danger for you and the kitten. Likewise, never leave an iron on its board. Should you be called to the telephone, you can just bet that this will be the time that kitty will decide to climb the trailing wire and cause the iron to tumble over. All open and electrical fireplaces should, of course, be fitted with a mesh guard.

If you keep fish, be sure the tank hood is secure so that the kitten cannot knock it off and fall in the water. Indoor plants are best kept well out of kitty's reach. Apart from damaging them, some could prove poisonous if the leaves were nibbled. Any cherished ornaments should also be placed well away from a kitten.

SLEEPING ARRANGEMENTS

Your kitten will be happy to sleep anywhere that is cozy, warm, and draft-free. This can be in a cat basket; its carrier, in which a soft blanket has been placed; on a chair; or best of all, on your bed. If you are the kind of person who does not look kindly on cats sleeping on your chairs or other furniture, the best advice I can give you is to forget about owning a cat!

If you wish to restrict the rooms where your cat may sleep, the simple solution is to be sure the doors are closed to those rooms. If you allow your kitten to sleep on your bed, do this only if you intend to let it do so once it is grown up; otherwise, it is unfair. Kittens really love sleeping with their owners, and they are no trouble at all—quite the opposite. They will amuse you with their antics.

LITTER TRAINING

Cats are extremely clean and fastidious in all aspects of their

Good grooming habits should start at an early age. Your pet shop can help you select the proper grooming aids for your cat. Photo courtesy of the Kong Company.

personal habits. Kittens are easily litter box trained, providing certain fundamentals are observed. The first of these is that cats do not like to attend to their toiletry needs in an already fouled litter box. Be sure fecal matter is always removed once you see that the kitten has used the litter box. Disinfect the litter box every few days so that it does not become smelly.

Litter training is accomplished simply by placing the kitten in the litter box every time it looks as though it wants to relieve itself. Such times will be whenever it wakes up, after it has eaten, and after it has been playing a while. One warning sign is the kitty turning in circles or searching for a corner while mewing.

Some cats like a place of their own to sleep, like a basket or a soft blanket. However, not all kittens are as lucky as this Himalayan, who has his own house and his own playmates.

Approach the kitten without alarming it and quickly transfer it to the litter box. Once this has been done on one or two occasions, the kitten will go to the litter box by itself. The main litter box is normally placed near the kitchen door. It is then a case of ensuring that it is kept clean. If the kitten roams freely indoors,

you can place another litter box at a strategic point. Never admonish a kitten should it make the odd mistake, as this will prove counterproductive. Rarely will such a situation occur with a litter-trained kitten, unless the youngster is feeling ill or has loose bowels. Remember, kittens can control their bowels only for a few seconds. Total control comes, as with humans, with maturity.

GENERAL TRAINING

Cats live for the moment; they do not relate the past with the present, but draw from it via their memory to determine a course of present action. An example will illustrate this point. If you call your pet to you and then discipline it for doing something in the past, whether this was minutes before or days before, the cat will relate only to what is happening at that moment.

Any discipline imposed out of context, i.e., the time and place of the offense, will be meaningless. Any discipline must therefore occur at the moment of the misdemeanor, otherwise the two things will not be connected in the mind of your Himalayan. If your cat is scratching the furniture, simply shout "no" if you cannot get to it and take it to the scratching post. It will associate the harsh "no" with the act of scratching the furniture, which is what you want. When you see it scratching its post, you praise it, and it will register in its mind that scratching this particular object pleases you. Training is as simple as that and only becomes difficult after a cat has been allowed to acquire bad habits.

CATS AND OTHER PETS

Kittens, in particular, will get along well with other cats and other pets if they are introduced to them at a young age. However, potential prey species are not included. Never leave a cat alone with a mouse, gerbil, hamster, small bird, baby rabbits, or guinea pigs. If it doesn't kill them, it will either maul them or frighten them. Where dogs are concerned, you must watch how the dog reacts and always be present until you know they are compatible.

When kittens are introduced into a home that already has an adult cat, the cat may be curious or hostile.

However, its hostility will only take the form of spitting at the kitten or maybe cuffing it around the head with a sheathed paw. How soon it accepts the kitten can range from hours to months. Some adults will become very friendly with a kitten as it matures, others will tolerate it without ever wishing to socialize too much. Always lavish extra praise on the resident pet so that it never becomes jealous of the new interloper.

Cats are very clean animals and don't like to use dirty litter boxes. Be sure to clean your Himalayan's box after you notice that it has been used and disinfect it every few days to prevent odor.

GROOMING

Daily, or at the least every other day, grooming is essential if you own a Himalayan or any other longhaired cat. If your pet is given access to the outdoors, the coat will become tangled and matted

When grooming your Himalayan, comb the face very gently, as it is one of the most sensitive parts on its body. If you comb its sensitive areas too roughly, your Himalayan will not be enthusiastic about regular grooming.

feel a mat, do not pull at it but tease it apart with your fingers, then brush it, then comb again. Repeat this process until all of the hair has been groomed.

Now you can use your narrow-toothed comb to complete the grooming; do this in the same manner as with the other comb. Finish with a brisk brushing. Always take special care when combing down the legs, the tail, and the underbelly, as they are especially sensitive parts. Your pet will resent any undue pressure on them. Brush and comb the face carefully and very gently.

While grooming, take the opportunity to inspect the skin, the ears, teeth, and between the paws. In the skin, you are looking

While grooming your Himalayan, inspect the eyes, ears, teeth, and paws very carefully. Because the Himalayan has a foreshortened muzzle, it is prone to blocked tear ducts that cause runny eyes.

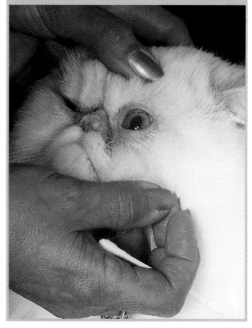

without daily grooming. Remember, a long coat is not natural for a cat. Burrs, grasses, leaves, and any number of foreign bodies will cling to a long coat and be the source of problems. Cuts, sores, and lumps are not easily seen in a Himalayan and can escape your attention unless you are grooming on a regular basis.

Begin as soon as you obtain your kitten. This will soon become a familiar event to the kitty. Providing you go about it in a gentle manner, it should become a pleasurable experience. Always begin by using your brush with the lie of the fur and then against it. This removes any objects in the fur and untangles the coat. Next use the wide-toothed comb. If you

After time, your Himalayan should get along with other pets, especially if they are raised together from youth. However, small rodent-like pets (hamsters, rats, guinea pigs, etc.) should not be left alone with any cat!

Proper and careful grooming can help prevent mats from forming and will keep your Himalayan's coat looking healthy and shiny.

for parasites, such as fleas or lice, or for cuts and abrasions. In the paw pads, you are looking for sores or any foreign bodies that might cause an abscess. When your Himalayan has a bath, it might be useful to have another family member help you. Be very sure that the cat has been well groomed before it is bathed; otherwise, mats will form that are better cut off. Be sure the water is only lukewarm, never hot or cold. Avoid getting shampoo in the ears or eyes. Use a shampoo formulated for cats.

Soak the hair thoroughly, then rub in the shampoo. Make sure that all the shampoo is rinsed from the coat; otherwise, it might irritate the skin when it dries. In any case, dry shampoo in the coat will make it sticky and will result in a lackluster appearance rather than a silky sheen. Finally, give the cat a brisk toweling, let it dry in a warm environment, and then groom it to remove any tangles that may have formed.

HANDLING CATS

If you have children, it is most important that they are instructed in the correct way to handle and appreciate their new pet. First of all, the kitten's privacy must be respected. Never let children wake up a sleeping kitten, because the kitty needs its sleep just as children do. Never let children play too roughly with a kitten, nor for an extended period of time. Cats like to play in short bursts. Always be sure that children never place elastic bands or string around the neck of a kitten, and never allow children to engage in a pulling match when a kitty has hold of a piece of string. This could get caught on their fragile teeth and damage or even pull one out.

The correct way to lift a kitten is to place your hand underneath its chest. Next you can place your free

These ten-week-old kittens are ready to go to their new home. Some breeders will keep their kittens until they are 12-16 weeks old.

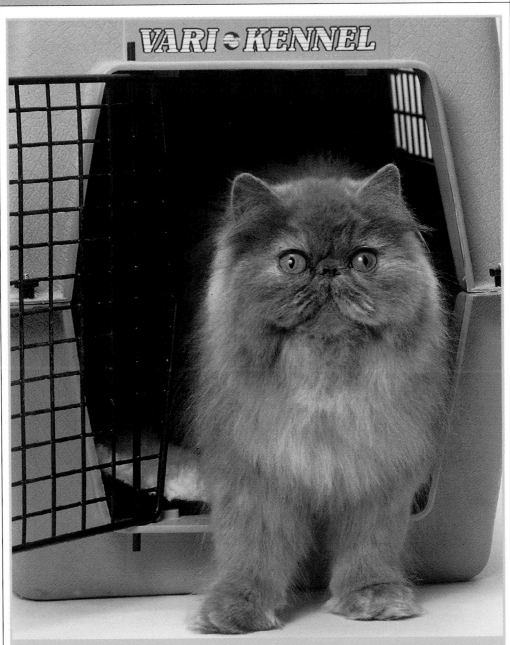

When traveling to the veterinarian, shows, or anywhere by motor vehicle, you should always put your Himalayan in a travel crate. Never allow pets to roam free in the car!

hand on its neck, throat, or shoulders to secure it. It can now be lifted and firmly but gently held to your chest while the hand securing its neck will be free to stroke it. A kitten or cat must never be lifted by its front legs, nor by the loose fur on its neck. When placing a kitten back on the floor, be sure it is held securely until it is at ground level. If it feels insecure, it will try to jump. In the process, it could scratch you and hurt itself if it lands awkwardly.

FEEDING YOUR HIMALAYAN

Cats and kittens are very much like people when it comes to their eating habits. Some are extremely easy to satisfy; others are much more difficult to please. Adult cats can be a worry, but at least you know they must have eaten something to have survived to maturity. Kittens, on the other its most difficult early months.

CATS ARE CARNIVORES

The cat is a prime predator in its wild habitat, and this means its basic diet must be composed of the flesh of other animals, be they mammals, birds, or fish. The digestive tract of a carnivore has

A Himalayan next to a bowl of fruit makes a pretty picture, but a cat will likely turn up its nose at fruits and vegetables as part of its diet. Meat, poultry, and fish are much more palatable to the carnivorous cat.

hand, can prematurely turn your hair gray because you fear they may not thrive unless you can come up with some delicacy that tempts their palate!

Fortunately, there are so many quality brands of commercial cat foods available today that it should be possible to get even the most fastidious of kittens through evolved to cope with proteins, but it has little ability to digest raw vegetable matter. This means the latter must first be boiled, so that the hard cellulose walls of such foods are softened, then broken down by the digestive juices and flora found in the alimentary tract.

In the wild, the cat would eat

Your Himalayan cat will enjoy human food in addition to its regular meals. These foods provide good exercise for its jaw as well as variety in its diet.

just about every part of its prey, leaving only the bones that were too large for it to digest. This diet would provide proteins and fats from the body tissues, roughage from the fur or feathers, and carbohydrates and vitamins from the partially digested vegetable matter that would be in the intestines of the prey. Combined with water, a very well-balanced diet would be provided for the cat. An equivalent of such nutrition is what you must strive to supply.

COMMERCIAL FOODS

Commercial cat foods encompass canned, semi-moist, and dry diets. The canned and dry foods come in an extensive range of flavors.

Commercial foods can form the basis of your Himalayan's diet, but you should supply a variety of them to reduce the chances that some key constituent is missing from the diet. You will find that some cats enjoy fish flavors, others poultry and yet others, the various meats.

Dry food is enjoyed by most, though not all, Himalayans. It provides good exercise for the teeth and jaw muscles, which canned foods do not. Their other advantage is that you can leave them out all day without their losing their appeal to your pets, or attracting flies. Water must always be available to your cats; this is even more important if the basic diet is of dried foods.

NON-COMMERCIAL FOODS

Your Himalayan will enjoy many of the foods that you eat. These foods provide both variety and good

Treats can be provided on an occasional basis to help provide a little variety in the diet. Some treats act as a cleansing agent to help reduce tartar on the cat's teeth. Photo courtesy of Heinz.

exercise for the jaws. Human consumption meats can be of beef, pork, or lamb. All fish should be steamed or boiled, and it is best to stay with white fish such as cod. Tuna, sardines, and other canned fish are appreciated, but only give small quantities of them as a treat because they may prove too rich for your pet's system. Chicken is enjoyed by nearly all cats.

Cheese, egg yolk, spaghetti, and even boiled rice are all items that you can offer to your pets to see if it appeals to them. Small beef and other meat bones that still have some meat on them will be enjoyed and keep a kitten or cat amused for quite some time. Beware of bones that easily splinter, such as those of chicken or rabbit.

You can by all means see if small pieces of vegetables or fruits are accepted if mixed with the food, but generally cats will leave them. This is no problem providing that the cat is receiving commercial foods as its basic diet. Such products are all fortified with essential vitamins after the cooking process.

HOW MUCH TO FEED?

Cats prefer to eat a little but often, rather than consume one mighty meal a day. However, as carnivores, adults are well able to cope with one large meal a day. The same is not true of kittens, which should receive three or four meals per day. A kitten or a cat will normally only consume that which is needed. You can arrive at this amount by trial and error. If kitty devours its meal and is looking for more, then let it have more. You will quickly be able to judge how much each kitten needs to satisfy itself. Always remove any moist foods that are uneaten after each meal.

At 12 weeks of age the kitten should have four meals a day. One of these meals can be omitted when the kitten is 16 weeks old, but increase the quantity of the other three. You can reduce to two meals a day when the kitten is about nine months of age. From that age, it is best to continue feeding two meals—one in the morning and one in the early evening. How many times a day you feed your adult cat is unimportant. The key factor is that it receives as much as it needs over the day, and that the diet is balanced to provide the

Giving your Himalayan a variety of flavors in its diet will keep it from becoming a picky eater and/or bored with its food. Canned foods come in many flavors, including beef, poultry, and fish.

essential ingredients discussed earlier. It is also better that meals are given regularly. Cats, like humans, are creatures of habit.

WATER

If a cat's diet is essentially of moist foods, it will drink far less than if the diet is basically of dry foods. Many cats do not like faucet (tap) water because they are able to smell and taste the many additives included by your local water board. Chlorine is high on this list. Although it dissipates into the air quite readily, chloromides do not, which is why the cat may ignore the water. During the filtering process at the water station, chemicals are both taken out and added. The resulting mineral balance and taste is often not to a cat's liking. This is why you will see cats drinking from puddles, a flower vase, or even your toilet, because the taste is better for them. If your water is refused, then you can see if your cat prefers mineralized bottled water—not distilled because the latter has no mineral content to it.

THE NEW ARRIVAL

It is a very traumatic time for a kitten when it leaves its mother and siblings. It will often eat well the first day; however, as it starts

Time to eat? Cats often become conditioned to the sound of a can opening or a box of food shaking—this Himalayan licks its lips in anticipation of feeding time.

This Himalayan kitten is ready to eat! He's got *almost* everything he needs—where's the food?

to miss its family, it will fret. You can reduce its stress by providing the diet it was receiving from the seller. You can change the diet slowly, if necessary, as it settles down. Of course, many kittens have no problems, but if yours does, this feeding advice should help its period of adjustment.

What is essential is that the kitten takes in sufficient liquids so that it does not start to dehydrate. This, more than anything else, will adversely affect its health very rapidly. If you are at all concerned, do consult your vet. The kitten may have picked up a virus, but if it is treated promptly, this should not be a problem. Your vet might supply you with a dietary supplement, which we have found excellent for kittens experiencing "new home syndrome."

YOUR HIMALAYAN'S HEALTH

Like any other animal, your Himalayan can fall victim to hundreds of diseases and conditions. Most can be prevented by sound husbandry. The majority, should they be recognized in their early stages, can be treated with modern drugs or by surgery. Clearly, preventive techniques are better and less costly than treatments, yet in many instances a cat will become ill because the owner has neglected some basic aspect of general management. In this chapter, we are not so much concerned with cataloging all the diseases your cat could contract, because these are legion, but more concerned with reviewing sound management methods.

HYGIENE

Always apply routine hygiene to all aspects of your pet's management. This alone dramatically reduces the chances of your pet becoming ill because it restricts pathogens (disease-causing organisms) from building up colonies that are able to overcome the natural defense mechanisms of your Himalayan.

1. After your cat has eaten its fill of any moist foods, either discard the food or keep it for

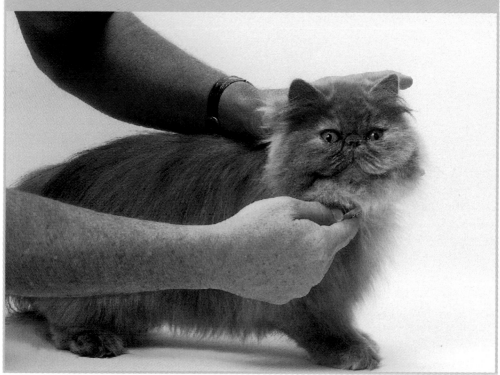

A major step in keeping your Himalayan cat healthy is regular grooming. Inspecting and brushing your cat at least every other day prevents fleas, ticks, and sores from going unnoticed.

Knowing your Himalayan's moods and actions will help you to determine if your cat is well or not. Being able to recognize any signs of a problem is invaluable to your cat's health.

later by placing it in your refrigerator. Anything left uneaten at the end of the day can be trashed. Always wash the bowl after each meal. Do not feed your pet from any dishes that are chipped, cracked, or, in the case of plastic, those that are badly scratched.

2. Always store food in a dry, cool cupboard or in the refrigerator in the case of fresh foods.

3. For whatever reason, if you have been handling someone else's cats, always wash your hands before handling your own cats.

4. Be rigorous in cleaning your cat' s litter box as soon as you see that it has been fouled.

5. Pay particular attention to the grooming of a Himalayan cat because so many problems can begin with a seemingly innocuous event. For example, in itself, a minor cut may not be a major problem as long as it is treated with an antiseptic. But if it is left as an open untreated wound, it is an obvious site for bacterial colonization. The bacteria then gain access to the bloodstream, and a major problem ensues that might not even be associated with the initial wound. The same applies to flea or lice bites. Inspect the skin carefully for signs of flea droppings when you groom

a Himalayan. These appear like minute specks of black dust.

RECOGNIZING AN ILL CAT

You must be able to recognize when your cat is ill in order to seek a solution to the problem. You must learn to distinguish between a purely temporary condition and that which will need some form of veterinary advice and/or treatment. For example, a cat can sprain a muscle by jumping and landing awkwardly. This would normally correct itself over a 36-48 hour period. Your pet may contract a slight chill, or its feces might become loose. Both conditions will normally correct themselves over a day or so. On the other hand, if a condition persists for more than two days, it would be advisable to telephone your vet for advice.

In general, any appearance or behavior that is not normal for your cat would suggest something is responsible for the abnormality. This is your first indication that something may be amiss. The following are a number of signs that indicate a problem:

1. Diarrhea, especially if it is very liquid, foul-smelling or blood-streaked. If blood is seen in the urine, this is also an indication of a problem, as is excessive straining or cries of pain when the cat tries to relieve itself.

2. Discharge from the nose or eyes. Many Himalayans may discharge a liquid from the eyes due to blocked tear ducts. This is associated with the foreshortening of the muzzle. However, an excessive discharge needs veterinary attention.

3. Repeated vomiting. All cats are sick occasionally with indigestion. They will also vomit after eating grass, but repeated vomiting is not normal.

4. Wheezing sounds when breathing, or any other suggestion of breathing difficulties.

5. Excessive scratching. All cats will have a good scratch on a quite regular basis, but excessive scratching indicates a skin

One sign that your Himalayan may be ill is if it is displaying a lack of interest in its favorite foods.

Keeping your Himalayan happy requires loving attention and regular interaction. Petting your Himalayan daily is good for your cat and can be therapeutic for you.

problem, especially if it has created sores or lesions.

6. Constant rubbing of the rear end along the ground.

7. Bald patches, lesions, cuts, and swellings on the body, legs, tail, or face.

8. The coat seems to lack bounce or life, and is dull.

9. The cat is listless and lethargic, showing little interest in what is going on around it.

10. The eyes have a glazed look to them, or the haw (nictitating membrane, or third eyelid) is clearly visible.

11. The cat is displaying an unusual lack of interest in its favorite food items.

12. The gums of the teeth seem very red or swollen.

13. Fits or other abnormal signs of behavior.

14. Any obvious pain or distress.

Very often two or more clinical signs will be apparent when a condition is developing. The number of signs increases as the disease or ailment advances to a more sinister stage.

DIAGNOSIS

Correct diagnosis is of the utmost importance before any form of treatment can be administered. Often it will require blood and/or fecal microscopy in order to establish the exact cause of a condition. Many of the signs listed above are common to most diseases, so never attempt home

An alert expression and a lustrous coat are two signs of a healthy Himalayan.

diagnosis and treatment: if you are wrong, your cherished Himalayan may pay for your error with its life. Once ill health is suspected, any lost time favors the pathogens and makes treatment both more difficult and more costly.

In making your original decision to purchase a Himalayan, or any other cat, you should always have allowed for the cost of veterinary treatment. If this is likely to be a burden that you cannot afford, then do not purchase a cat. The first few months, and especially the first weeks, is the time when most cats will become ill. If they survive this period, the chances are that future visits to the vet will be rare, other than for booster vaccinations.

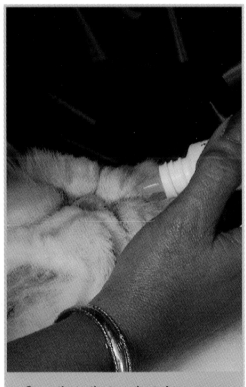

Sometimes the tear ducts become so blocked that veterinary treatment is required.

Kittens do not have the immunity to pathogens that the adult cat does, nor do they have the muscle reserves of the adult. If they are ill, they need veterinary help very quickly if they are to have a good chance of overcoming a disease or major problem.

Having decided that your cat is not well, you should make notes on paper of the signs of the problem, when you first noticed them, and how quickly things have deteriorated. If possible, obtain a fecal and urine sample, then telephone your vet and make an appointment. Ask other cat owners in your area who their vet is. Some vets display a greater liking for cats, or dogs, or horses than do others. This is just human nature, but obviously you want to go to one that has a special affection for felines.

TREATMENT

Once your vet has prescribed a course of treatment, it is important that you follow it exactly as instructed. Do not discontinue the medicine because the cat shows a big improvement. Such an action could prove counterproductive, and the pathogens that had not been killed might develop an immunity to the treatment. A relapse could occur, and this might be more difficult to deal with.

VACCINATIONS

There are a few extremely

To help keep your Himalayan sitting pretty, have regular checkups performed and stay current on all vaccination shots.

dangerous diseases that afflict cats, but fortunately there are vaccines that can dramatically reduce the risk of them infecting your Himalayan. The bacteria and viruses that cause such diseases are often found in the air wherever there are cats. Discuss a program of immunization with your vet.

When a kitten is born, it inherits protection from disease via the colostrum of its mother's milk. Such protection may last for up to 16 weeks—but it varies from kitten to kitten and may last only six weeks. It is therefore recommended that your kitten be vaccinated against diseases at six to eight weeks of age just to be on the safe side. Boosters are required some weeks later and thereafter each year. Potential breeding females should be given boosters about three to four weeks prior to the due date. This will ensure that a high level of antibodies is passed to the kittens.

An important consideration with regard to the major killer diseases in cats is the treatment of infection. If a cat survives an infection, it will probably be a carrier of the disease and shed the pathogens continually throughout its life. The only safe course is therefore to ensure that your kittens are protected. The main diseases for which there are vaccinations are as follows:

Rabies: This is a disease of the neurological system. It is non-existent in Great Britain, Ireland, Australia, New Zealand, Hawaii, certain oceanic islands, Holland, Sweden, and Norway. In these countries, extremely rigid quarantine laws are applied to ensure it stays that way. You cannot have your cat vaccinated against rabies if you live in one of these countries, unless you are about to emigrate with your cat. In all other countries, rabies vaccinations are either compulsory or strongly advised. They are given when the kitten is three or more months of age.

Feline panleukopenia: Also known as feline infectious enteritis, and feline distemper. This is a highly contagious viral disease. Vaccinations are given when the kitten is about eight weeks old, and a booster is given four weeks later. In high-risk areas, a third injection may be advised four weeks after the second one.

Feline respiratory disease complex: Often referred to as cat flu but this is incorrect. Although a number of diseases are within this group, two of them are especially dangerous. They are feline viral rhinotracheitis (FVR) and feline calicivirus (FCV). The vaccination for the prevention of these diseases is combined and given when the kitten is six or more weeks of age; a booster follows three to four weeks later.

Feline leukemia virus complex (FeLV): This disease was first recognized in 1964, and a vaccine became available in the US in about 1985. Like "cat flu," the name is misleading, because it is far more complex than a blood cancer, which is what its name implies. Essentially, it destroys the cat' s immune system, so the cat may contract any of the major

The Himalayan's long, thick coat can give fleas and ticks a place to hide. Thoroughly checking the coat on a regular basis is a major step in preventing infestation.

diseases.

The disease is easily spread via the saliva of a cat as it licks other cats. It is also spread prenatally from an infected queen to her offspring via the blood, or when washing her kittens. This is why it is important to test all breeding cats for FeLV. Vaccination is worthwhile only on a kitten or cat that has tested negative. If a cat tests positive for the disease, it has a 70 percent chance of survival, though it will be a carrier in many instances.

Feline infectious peritonitis (FIP): This disease has various effects on the body's metabolism. There are no satisfactory tests for it, but intranasal liquid vaccinations via a dropper greatly reduce the potential for it to develop in the tissues of the nose.

PARASITES

Parasites are organisms that live on or in a host. They feed from it without providing any benefit in return. External parasites include fleas, lice, ticks, flies, and any other creature that bites the skin of the cat. Internal parasites include all pathogens, but the term is more commonly applied to worms in their various forms.

External parasites and their eggs can be seen with the naked eye. All can be eradicated with treatment from your vet. However, initial treatment will need to be followed by further treatments because most compounds are ineffective on the eggs. The repeat treatments kill the larvae as they hatch. It is also important that all bedding be treated or destroyed

Owning a healthy Himalayan cat includes watching its weight as well as keeping it well groomed and nourished.

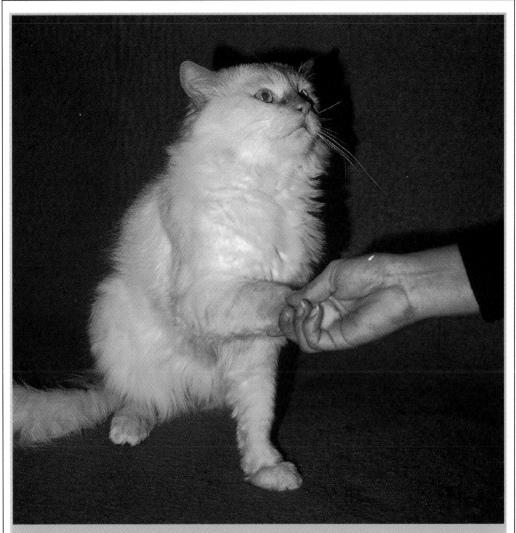

Regularly checking your Himalayan's foot pads and removing any dirt and debris will keep its feet clean and free of infection.

because this is often where parasites prefer to live when not on the host.

All cats are host to a range of worm species. If worms multiply in the cat, they adversely affect its health. They will cause loss of appetite, wasting, and a steady deterioration in health. At a high level of infestation, they may be seen in the fecal matter, but normally it will require fecal microscopy by your vet. This will establish the species and the relative density of the eggs, thus the level of infestation.

Treatment is normally via tablets, but liquids are also available. Because worms are so common, the best husbandry technique is to routinely treat breeding cats for worms prior to their being bred, then for the queen and her kittens to be treated periodically. Discuss a testing and treatment program with your vet.

NEUTERING AND SPAYING

Desexing your cat is normally done when a female is about four months of age and somewhat later with a male. The operation is quite simple with a male but more complicated with a female. It is still a routine procedure. It is possible to delay estrus in a breeding queen, but the risk of negative side effects makes this a dubious course to take. Discuss it with your vet. A cat of any age can be neutered (male) or spayed (female); but if they are adults, they take some months (especially males) before they lose their old habits.

FIRST AID

Although you might think that such inquisitive creatures as cats would be prone to many physical injuries, this is not actually the case. They usually extricate themselves from dangerous situations because of their very fast reflexes. However, injuries do happen, and the most common is caused by the cat darting across a road and being hit by a vehicle. About 40 percent of cats die annually due to traffic accidents. The next level of injury will be caused by cats getting bitten or scratched when fighting among themselves, or being bitten by an insect, or by a sharp object getting lodged in their fur or feet.

If your cat is hit by a vehicle, the first thing to do is to try and place it on a board of some sort and remove it to a safe place. Do not lift its head because this might result in it swallowing blood into the lungs. Try to keep it calm by talking soothingly to it.

If the cat is still mobile, but has clearly been badly hurt, you must try and restrict its movements by wrapping it in a blanket or towel. If it is bleeding badly, try to contain the flow by wrapping a bandage around the body or leg to reduce the blood loss. With a minor cut, you should trim the hair away from the wound, bathe it, then apply an antiseptic or stem the flow with a styptic pencil or other coagulant.

If you suspect that your cat has been bitten by an insect and the result is a swelling, the poison is already in the skin so external ointments will have virtually no effect. The same is true of an abscess caused by fighting. The only answer is to let your vet use surgery to lance and treat the wound.

Fortunately, cats rarely swallow poison because they are such careful eaters. In all instances, immediately contact your vet and advise him of the kind of poison the cat has consumed.

If your cat should ever be badly frightened, for example, by a dog chasing and maybe biting it, the effect of this may not be apparent immediately. It may go into shock some time later. Keep the cat indoors so that you can see how it reacts. Should it go into shock and collapse, place a blanket around it and take it to the vet. If this is not possible, place it in a darkened room and cover it with a blanket so it does not lose too much body heat. Comfort it until you can make contact with the vet.

A Himalayan who receives good veterinary care and whose owner knows basic first aid procedures will be the picture of good health.

COLORS AND STANDARD

In order to cater to both the potential breeder and the pet owner, I have divided this chapter into three parts. The first is a description of the various colors presently seen in the Himalayan; this will meet the needs of breeder and pet owner. The second part discusses in simple terms how these colors are passed from one generation to another. This information will be indispensable to the breeder but may also interest the enthusiastic pet owner. The third part is the Himalayan standard, which is essential for exhibition.

THE HIMALAYAN PATTERN

The pattern of the Himalayan is the same as in the Siamese. The facial mask, the ears, the legs, and the tail are darker in color than the rest of the body. The face should display an obvious color mask that separates it from the ears. The body color is the same as that of the points yet a lighter shade. In some varieties, the color may shade from darker to lighter on the body, but in others, the body color should be as even as possible. In all colors, the nose leather, paw pads, and eye rims should tone with the points color.

The mask should cover an area that extends from above the eyes, around the whisker pads, and down to the chin. In lighter color varieties, the mask is less obvious than in darker colors and very often is not as extensive. This same remark applies to other parts of the pointed pattern that feature very light colors. In all instances, the eyes must be a very obvious blue, though in young kittens the eye color may be late in development. The full pigmentation in this breed may not be achieved until it is about 18 months of age.

White patches anywhere in the points is a bad fault, as is a lack of contrast between points and body color. Here again however, allowance must be made for the color in question because contrasts are more obvious in the

The Himalayan's mask should cover most of the face—above the eyes, around the whisker pads, and down to the chin.

darker varieties, such as the seal, than in the lightest shades, such as the lilac or the cream. The number of color varieties is greater in Britain than in the USA. This is in keeping with the general observation that the British recognize new colors sooner than their American cousins yet are more conservative when it comes to recognizing new breeds of cats.

HIMALAYAN COLORS

The following descriptions are of the ideal requirements, which are not easily attained, especially in respect to the "no shading" in those varieties where it should not be seen.

•*Seal Points:* are a deep seal brown. Body is a fawn shading to creamy white below.

•*Chocolate Points:* are a milk chocolate. Body is an ivory color displaying no shading.

•*Blue Points:* are blue. Body is a bluish (glacial) white shading to white on the underparts.

•*Lilac Points:* are a warm lilac (grayish-pink). Body is magnolia or glacial white with no shading.

•*Red (Flame) Points:* are a rich orange or red. Body is apricot or creamy white.

•*Cream Points:* are buff cream with no apricot. Body is creamy white with no shading.

•*Tortie Points:* are seen in the base colors of either seal, chocolate, blue, or lilac, which is broken with unbrindled shades of red or cream. Some red and/or cream is desirable on all the points. A facial blaze of red or cream is permissible (UK) or desirable (USA).

•*Tabby Points (also called Lynx point in the USA):* tabby markings are placed over the points. This means that the forehead will display the typical tabby "M" or scarab beetle mark. The legs and tail will feature broken rings or bracelets. The ears will show a "thumb" mark.

•*Seal Tabby:* Seal point markings on an

The Siamese cat's genes are what give the Himalayan its point pattern, which consists of the facial mask and the markings on the ears, the legs, and the tail.

pale brown agouti ground. Body is cream-white.

•*Chocolate Tabby:* Milk chocolate brown point markings on a light bronze agouti ground.

•*Blue Tabby:* Blue point markings on light beige ground. Body is glacial blue-white.

•*Lilac Tabby:* Lilac point markings on a pale beige ground. Body is magnolia white.

•*Red Tabby:* Rich-red point

The blue point Himalayan cat has a body with glacial (bluish) white to pure white shading on its underparts.

markings on a light apricot agouti ground. Body is apricot white.

•*Cream Tabby:* Cream point markings on a paler cream ground. Body is a tone lighter creamy white.

•*Tortie-Tabby Point:* the normal tabby pattern is overlaid with red and/or cream. The amount of the tortie areas present is not important as long as both elements of the pattern, tortie and tabby, are clearly visible. Presently, the tortie-tabby point is available in seal, chocolate, blue-cream, and lilac-cream.

In cats, the tortie (tortoiseshell) pattern is a female sex-limited feature (other than in genetically abnormal males, which are extremely rare and invariably sterile). The tortie and the tortie-tabby point colors are therefore limited to females. Blue-cream is

the diluted form of tortie (black and red), so all blue-cream felines are thus females. At this time, there are some 20 colors for you to choose from in the Himalayan breed. Allowing for natural variation in the depth of colors, the potential is almost unlimited.

THE GENETICS OF PATTERN

The theory of genetics just explained can now be applied to the color pattern of the Himalayan. At another of the gene loci is a gene pair that controls the amount of color that can be formed in the coat. It is known as the full-color locus and is identified as *C*. It is sometimes called the albino locus *A* because its extreme alternative recessive mutant gene prevents any color from being formed. Such a cat (rare) would have the genotype of *aa*. However, between full color and no color there are three other alternative expressions. One is

GC New Wave Andromeda, a red (or flame) point Himalayan owned by Anne T. Wilson, is a proven gem.

Burmese, the second is Siamese, while the third is a blue-eyed white. A full-colored, non-tabby cat would be black. If the Burmese gene is present in double dose, the black is reduced to dark brown but with some paler color being present on the body.

In the Siamese pattern, the dark brown is restricted to the points, while the body color is paler. This gene is identified as c^s, so the Himalayan has the pattern genotype of $c^s c^s$ (one gene on each of a pair of chromosomes) making it a Siamese. Do understand that, genetically, Siamese is a color pattern not a specific breed type, unless it is stated in a genetic text. Now, a non-pointed Persian cat does not carry any Siamese

The typical "M" or scarab beetle mark of the seal lynx point is where Himalayan Purrmates' Devine Miss M gets her name. Owned by Elizabeth Stamper.

Because the tortie pattern in cats is female sex-limited, all blue cream (the diluted form of tortie, which is black and red) tortie-tabby pointed Himalayans are female. Owned by Janet Whitman.

genes, so it has the genotype of CC. When the Himalayan is paired to the non-pointed Persian to maintain type, as is quite common, the formulae will be: CC x $c^s c^s = Cc^s$.

This is the only potential combination of the genes that each parent can pass to their offspring. All of the kittens are therefore non-pointed Persians but carry the Himalayan gene. If one of these kittens is paired to a Himalayan, the formulae will be: Cc^s x $c^s c^s = Cc^s$ $C^s c^s$ $c^s c^s$ $c^s c^s$.

Translated, this means there will be 50% Persian pointed carriers and 50% pure bred Himalayans. If the carriers are paired to each other, the result will be: Cc^s x $Cc^s = CC$ Cc^s $c^s C$ $c^s c^s$.

This results in 25% pure non-pointed Persians, 50% Persian pointed carriers, and 25% pure Himalayans. The non-pointed have no Himalayan in them whatsoever, which makes them pure Persian in their color (whatever that might be). These various matings indicate to you just how useful a genetic knowledge is to the Himalayan breeder.

THE GENETICS OF COLORS

Color, along with all other features of your Himalayan, is passed from one generation to another via tiny units of coded information known as genes. These genes act in a very predictable manner, so you can work out what colors will result from given matings—as long as you know what sort of color genes your cats have to start with.

Unlike colors created by paints that are mixed, genes never blend and always retain their individual identity or expression. Colors in cats can therefore be created and removed by manipulating them during reproduction.

The genes are arranged in a linear manner along threads known as chromosomes. The chromosomes are always paired and, other than in the sex cells, are of the same length. This means that at every gene locus (site) there is another gene of the same type on the opposite of a pair of chromosomes. During reproduction the paired chromosomes are parted. One each of the original pair of chromosomes of each parent passes to the offspring, which thus are born with their own pair.

There are many gene loci that control color. Depending on what information each gene contains will determine what color and pattern a cat displays. For example, we known there are at least 20 gene loci in domestic cats. This is known because when a gene suddenly alters the way it expresses itself, which is called a mutation, it can be identified and named. The interaction of all of these differing expressions gives us all of the color patterns and fur types seen in cats.

The genes do not have the same power of expression. For our basic purposes these genes can be divided into two types: dominant and recessive. The former will always mask the presence of the latter if one of each type is found at a particular gene locus. This means that for recessive genes to be visually seen, they must be present on both chromosomes of a pair. In other words, they must be in double dose.

Let us take the longhair of the Himalayan as an example. The normal (wild) cat coat is shorthaired. The gene that controls it is identified as *L*. It is given a capital letter to indicate it is of a dominant type. When genetics became a studied science, the feline longhaired gene was found to be recessive to short hair and was given the letter *l* to indicate it was of the recessive type. It was the mutant alternative gene expression of the normal wild type at that locus. Note the hair gene is named for the mutant gene, thus the shortcoated hair gene is *L*. Each feature has at least a pair of genes (one on each chromosome) that controls it, so a shorthaired cat can have the genotype of *Ll* or *LL*. Both look the same yet will breed different depending on the genotype of their mate. For example, if an *Ll* cat mated one of the same type, the mating would have the formulae of: *Ll x Ll = LL Ll ll ll.*

You must work out all possible combinations of the genes that each parent can pass to their offspring. Of this litter the theoretical expectations would be three (75%) shorthaired kittens and one (25%) longhaired.

One of the shorthaired (*LL*) would be pure bred for its hair type, while the other two (*Ll*) would not, but you could not distinguish the genotypes from visual appearance, only by breeding with them. The longhaired youngster, being a double recessive, is pure bred for its hair. The two shorthaired kittens with the single but unseen *l* genes are called shorthaired split for longhair, which is written as shorthair/longhair. The former is visual, but the latter is not. Another way of describing such a kitten is to say it is a longhair carrier. Do bear in mind that the expectations are theoretical and would be accurate over large numbers of litters but not necessarily in a single litter due to the random way in which the potential gene combinations could become a reality.

Having looked at the hair length and the pattern of the Himalayan, we can end by looking at the colors themselves. This is straight forward but a little more complex, so you need to think carefully about what is happening. Another gene locus controls the amount of melanin (a dark pigment) that the coat can contain. It is identified as *B* in the normal coat, and its mutant alternative is *b*, which reduces its strength so that the normal black color (but very dark brown in the Siamese) becomes a lighter shade—that known as chocolate (brown). At yet another locus is a gene that determines the density of the pigment present, which is identified with the letter *D* and is derived from its mutant alternative *d* that dilutes the density.

We now have the means to genetically identify all of the solid non-sex-linked colors in the breed, which are as follows: Sealpoint—c^sc^s, Blue—c^sc^sdd, Chocolate—c^sc^sbb, and Lilac (Frost)—c^sc^sbbdd.

If any Himalayans with these colors are mated to their own genotype, they will breed true to their color. But what if they are interbred? We will pair a blue with a chocolate. The Siamese gene can be ignored because this is obviously common to both the parents, so the offspring will automatically be Himalayan marked. The formulae will thus be: $bbDD \times BBdd = bBDd$.

This is the only permutation the offspring can inherit. The result, translated to color, is 100% sealpoint, which neither parent was. We must, however, add that the kittens are sealpoint/chocolate-dilute, meaning sealpoint split for both the chocolate and the dilute mutations. How did the sealpoint arise? First, note that in writing the genotype of the chocolate, I indicated its genotype at the dilute locus as well. This is most important. At that locus it is DD for normal or full-color density expression. Likewise, the blue point is normal BB at the brown locus, which is called chocolate in this breed.

When the genes from each parent combine to produce the $bBDd$ combination, the resulting color becomes apparent. At the B locus the dominant B for dark brown masks the other gene b of that pair, so the color is seal — the darkest of the browns. Likewise at the density locus, the normal full density D masks the presence of the dilute mutant d, so the dark brown (seal) displays

Genetics determine a cat's coat color, and Himalayans are seen in a variety of colors. This is a blue point Himalayan owned by Janet Whitman.

The Himalayan cat's head should be round and massive with great breadth of skull. This seal tortie-tabby has a well-structured head.

The Himalayan is one of the most popular show cats because of its outstanding color and gentle temperament. Owned by Elizabeth and Homer Stamper.

its full-color intensity. All of these kittens are carrying the *b* and *d* mutations, which will influence the color of their own offspring depending on the genotype of their chosen partner.

If a breeder with no genetic knowledge purchased and mated two of these sealpoints, they would no doubt be very surprised to find other colors emerging in the subsequent litter. They might be delighted — or very annoyed if they wished to specialize in sealpoints! The importance of knowing your Himalayans genotype is thus very beneficial if you plan to breed. If you are unsure of a given gene's status when writing a genotype, you should place a dash to represent it. Thus a shorthaired cat might be denoted as *L-*, which indicates the status of the other gene is unknown at that time. A seal point would be *D-* at the density locus because it could be *DD* or *Dd*. Once the status is known it can be included in the cat's records.

Space, unfortunately, does not allow for discussion of sex-linked red and its dilution the cream, which create the tortie. With respect to the tabby point, any calculations you wish to make that include this pattern should be preceded by the letters *AA* to indicate the tabby and *aa* to indicate the non-tabby or solid colorpoint. The letters actually stand for agouti and non agouti, with the normal agouti (tabby) being dominant to the non agouti. All cats are obligate tabbies! The only reason you see blacks, whites, Himalayans, and all other colors and patterns is because these others all carry the recessive gene for non agouti in double dose in their genotype. This makes them black cats. From that point, the many other mutations, some of which we have discussed, will change this to blue, brown, red, white, and so on by their presence, absence, or interaction. The subject is quite fascinating and at times very frustrating.

THE HIMALAYAN STANDARD

The following standard is that of the Cat Fanciers Association(CFA) of the USA. The CFA regards the Himalayan as a pointed Persian, so I have omitted a small reference in the first part of the standard that deals with bi-color and other "with white" varieties, which is not applicable to the Himalayan.

Head—round and massive with great breadth of skull. Round face with round underlying bone structure. Well set on a short, thick neck.

Nose—short, snub, and broad. With "break" centered between the eyes.

Cheeks—full

Jaws—broad and powerful.

Chin—full, well developed, and firmly rounded, reflecting a proper bite.

Ears—small, round tipped, tilted forward, and not unduly open at the base. Set far apart and low on the head, fitting into (without distorting) the rounded contour of the head.

Eyes—brilliant in color, large,

round, and full. Set level and far apart, giving a sweet expression to the face.

Body—of cobby type, low on the legs, deep in the chest, equally massive across the shoulders and rump, with a short, well-rounded middle piece. Good muscle tone with no evidence of obesity. Large or medium in size. Quality is the determining consideration rather than size.

Back—level.

Paws—large, round, and firm. Toes carried close, five in front and four behind.

Tail—short but in proportion to body length. Carried without a curve and at an angle lower than the back.

Coat—long and thick, standing off from the body. Of fine texture, glossy, and full of life. Long all over the body, including the shoulders. Ruff immense and continuing in a deep frill between the front legs. Ear and toe tufts long. Brush very full.

Disqualify—locket or button. Kinked or abnormal tail. Incorrect number of toes. Any apparent weakness in the hindquarters. Any apparent deformity of the spine. Deformity of the skull resulting in any asymmetrical face and/or head. Also disqualify for crossed eyes, white toes, eye color other than blue.

Two popular eye colors of the Himalayan cat are deep vivid blue and brilliant copper. Eyes should be full and set far apart.

EXHIBITING HIMALAYANS

From the first time cats were seriously exhibited in London in 1871, the cat show has been the very heart of the fancy. It is the place where breeders can have the merits of their stock assessed in a competitive framework, where all cat lovers can meet and discuss ideas, trends and needs, and where new products for cats can be promoted. It is the only event in which you have the opportunity of seeing just about every color and pattern variety that exists in the Himalayan breed.

Even if you have no plans to become a breeder or exhibitor, you should visit at least one or two cat shows to see what a quality Himalayan looks like.

Owning an award-winning championship Himalayan cat takes time, patience, and proper care. International Ch. Mingchiu Mandarin of Sahadi holds titles from England, Scotland, and Wales.

TYPES OF SHOW

Shows range from the small informal affairs that attract a largely local entry to the major all-breed championshipss and specialty exhibitions that can be spread over two or more days (but only one in Britain). A specialty is a show restricted either by breed or by hair length (short or long). In the US, it is quite common for two or more shows to run concurrently at the same site.

SHOW CLASSES

The number of classes staged at a given show will obviously reflect its size, but the classes fall into various major divisions. These are championships for whole cats, premierships for altered cats, open classes for both of the previous cats, kittens, and household pets. In all but the pet class, there are separate classes for males and females. There are then classes for all of the color and pattern varieties. At a small show, the color/patterns may be grouped into fewer classes than at a major show.

All classes are judged against the standard for the breed, other than pet classes, in which the exhibits are judged on the basis of condition and general appeal, or uniqueness of pattern. An unregistered Himalayan can be entered into a pet class, and it will be judged on the same basis as would a mixed breed. A kitten in the US is a cat of four months of age but under eight months on the day of a show. In Britain a kitten is a cat of three or more months and under nine months on the show day.

AWARDS AND PRIZES

The major awards in cats are those of Champion and Grand Champion, Premier and Grand Premier. In Britain, a cat must win three challenge certificates under different judges to become a champion, while in the US it must win six winner's ribbons. In both instances, these awards are won via the open class. Once a cat is a champion, it then competes in the champions' class and becomes a grand based on points earned in defeating other champions. The prizes can range from certificates, ribbons and cups to trophies and cash.

Wins in kitten classes do not count toward champion status. Champion status in one association does not carry over to another, in which a cat would have to win its title again based on the rules of that association. The rules of competition are complex, and any would-be exhibitor should obtain a copy of them from their particular registry.

The general format of cat shows, while differing somewhat from one country to another, are much the same in broad terms. A Himalayan will enter its color or pattern class. If it wins, it will progress to compete against the other group winners in its breed, and ultimately compete for best of breed. If classes have been scheduled for all of the recognized colors and patterns in all of the recognized breeds, then a Best in Show will be the ultimate award. The best in Show (BIS) award is the highest award that a cat can receive and the dream of every cat exhibitor.

JUDGING

As stated earlier, cats are judged against their written standard rather than against each other. A winning cat is one that records the highest total of points, or, put another way, the least number of demerit marks. In the US cats are taken to the judge's table for assessment, but in Britain the judge moves around the pens with a trolley. In the US, judging is done in front of the public, but in the UK judging is normally done before the public is allowed into the hall. The exhibit owners are requested to leave the hall during judging.

Some Himalayan cats can be trained to accomplish all sorts of feats. One such Himalayan is flame-pointed Tr. Ch. Red Sunset of Osso, owned by John W. and Sheelah M. Preusse.

Because of their relaxed nature, Himalayans are easy to train and judge, making them popular exhibition cats for owners and judges alike.

CAT PENS

When you arrive at the cat show, a pen will be allocated to your cat. This is an all-wire cage. In Britain, the rules governing what can be placed into the cage are very rigid. This is because there can be no means of identifying the owner of the cat when the judge arrives at that pen. Thus, the blanket, the litter box and the water vessel must all be white. In the US the pens are highly decorated with silks, gorgeous cushions, and so on because the cat is taken to another pen for judging.

THE EXHIBITION HIMALAYAN

Obviously, a Himalayan show cat must be a very sound example of its breed. Its coat must be in truly beautiful condition because the level of competition is extremely high at the major events. At more local affairs, the quality will not be as high, which gives more exhibitors a chance to pick up victories in the absence of the top cats of the country. The male cat must have two descended testicles and have a valid vaccination certificate against feline enteritis that was issued at least seven days before the show. It should have tested negative for feline leukemia (and/or any other diseases as required by your registry).

A show cat must be well-mannered because if it should bite or claw the judge, it is hardly likely to win favor. It could even be disqualified, depending on the regulations of your registry. In any case, such a cat could not be examined properly by the judge, so this alone would preclude it from any hope of winning. It must therefore become accustomed to such treatment by being handled very often as a kitten by friends and relatives.

ENTERING A SHOW

You must apply to the show secretary for an entry blank and a schedule. The secretary will list the classes and state the rules of that association. The entry form must be completed and returned, with fees due, by the last date of entry as stipulated for that show. It is very important that you enter the correct classes; otherwise, your cat will be eliminated and your fee forfeited. If you are unsure about this aspect, you can seek the advice of an exhibitor of your acquaintance, or simply call the show secretary, who will advise you.

SHOW ITEMS

When attending a show you will need a variety of items. They include a cat carrier, litter box, blankets, food and water vessels, food, your cat's own supply of your local water if necessary, disinfectant, first aid kit, grooming tools, paper towels, entry pass, vaccination certificates, show catalog to check the entry for your cat and when it is likely to be judged, a small stool, and decorations for the pen. You may also wish to take your own food. Indeed, it would be wise to invest in a collapsible cart or trolley to transport all of the above!

The best advice is that you should visit shows and talk with exhibitors so that you can get the feel of things before you make the plunge yourself. Showing is a fascinating and thoroughly addictive pastime, but it is also time-consuming, can be costly, and entails a great deal of dedication. Fortunately, you can participate to whatever level you wish. You are also assured of making many new friends in the process.

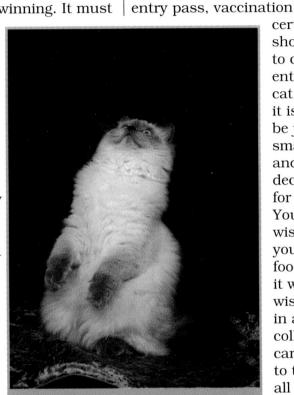

Pick me! A near-perfect (and very confident) Himalayan stands up to be noticed by a passing-by judge.